An Encourag

W
C.P. Rees, Bethesda, Narberth

Copyright © C P Rees 2019

First Published August 2019

ISBN 978-1-9995850-5-1

Designed, Printed & Published by Design Marque
Printed in Great Britain by www.designmarque.co.uk

Front cover Rebecca Tadman, Intercession
Scripture Reference NKJV

Dedication

This little booklet is dedicated to the faithful members who have been an encouragement with their prayers to the work of the Gospel here at Bethesda and especially not forgetting those in the past, whose presence at the prayer meeting and petitions are not forgotten before the throne of grace.

If we would understand the potential power of our prayers, we would be on our knees a hundred times a day and ask Him things that would turn the world upside down.

Brother Andrew

We must be careful not to break the habit of true prayer and imagine other works to be necessary, which after all are nothing of the kind.

Martin Luther

Of all Thy gifts we ask but one, we ask the constant power to pray indulge us, Lord in this request; Thou canst not then deny the rest.

C. Wesley

Prayer also will be made for Him continually,

And daily He shall be praised.

Psalm 72.15

Contents

Preface

Prayer is the one gift which each and every child of God possesses. Some may have the gift of preaching, others faith, another of ministry, another of mercy and another of administration but all have the gift of prayer. It is impossible to be a Christian without it, you received the *Spirit of adoption, by whom we cry out Abba Father.*[1] If you are the one talent Christian, the talent you possess is this one, do not bury it! Pray and learn all you can on how to use the gift God has given you; read everything the Bible says about prayer, note down the place and prominence it has in the practice and teaching of Jesus Christ. Prayer was a priority of Our Lord and Saviour even before the work of teaching and healing, [2] which is a humbling and convicting thought. If Jesus knew the need to draw aside for communion with His Heavenly Father in His life on earth, how much more do we in our walk with God!

Interestingly, the Lord Jesus never taught His disciples how to preach but He did teach them how to pray. It is also interesting that the disciples never asked the question teach us to *'preach'* but

---

1   Romans 8.15
2   Luke 4.42, 5.15-16.

teach us to *'pray.'* The Bible does not command us to *preach* without ceasing but to *pray* without ceasing.

The thoughts in this little pocket book have been gleaned from great prayer warriors. Spurgeon, referring to his sermons said, *"he collected from many different flowers but the honey made was his own."* The thoughts and Scriptures found in this little booklet hopefully will be used of the Holy Spirit to inspire, stimulate and guide to this great work. To be ever ready to intercede for others, better prepared to ask according to His will, present more acceptable petitions unto Him, to know answers to prayers which give God the glory, advance His kingdom and hasten the day for the return of Our Lord and Saviour Jesus Christ. The Church progresses on its knees and not so much through public efforts but on the prayers of the quiet faithful. May God the Father richly bless you in this glorious privilege that has been given to us with all spiritual blessing in Christ Jesus.

Yours in the Master's Service.

 C P Rees

Some thoughts using this Booklet

The knowledge of prayer is of the utmost importance and should be the foundational studies in the school of Christ.

This small booklet is not one about prayer, you can buy many such books on the market teaching, instructing and inspiring one to better praying with God. In this little booklet you will not find any prayers to pray, there are many such prayer books - *prayers for all seasons, for every day of the week, great prayers of the past,* but it is the belief of the writer, it's not so much written prayers on paper that God hears but those prayers written on the heart by the Holy Spirit Himself. If you want written prayers on paper to pray the best ones are found in His Word and please, please, pray THEM. This booklet is not a read from cover to cover, but rather something to turn to before prayer, hoping it may be a means to quicken the heart to call out to God and to give some added thought to the petitions we offer.

For example, in the chapter *Encouragement to*

Pray, which are verses given to us by God found in His Holy Word to stir us up to call upon Him in faith, to quote one Prayer Saint, *every promise in Scripture is a command to pray.* These verses are not exhaustive and you will find blank spaces in this little booklet to note down those verses that God has given you to pray through and space to note down some burdens on your heart, also room to record those gracious answers that He gives and to give Him praise.

Turn to those verses from God's Word that give faith to believe that God hears. Then also, to take a verse to pray when one feels dry and unable to come to Him, just one verse has brought forth many petitions. *Prayer brings heaven down to the soul and lifts the soul up to heaven.*

You will find some directions and practical points on prayer drawn from the Scriptures to this great work. It was the disciples of the Lord who asked Him the question *teach us to pray?* It is the deep longing of our hearts Lord *teach us to pray* and He has done so by showing us how He prayed, when

He prayed, the gestures He used and the places He offered supplication up to God. From every gesture He made and everything He said, from every prayer He made, the teaching He gave on the subject, we learn how to approach God.

Think for example the account we have of Paul praying on the beach, you may find yourself in such a place one day and the Holy Spirit will prompt you to make a petition to Him from such a place just like the Apostle, these little incidental things to us are mentioned here because they are not incidental to God, they are recorded in His book.

There are many little lessons to learn concerning this all-important work; when to continue in prayer, how to continue, the practice of prayer even when we do not feel like it. If you do not pray well in the morning think about it and try and pray with thought in the evening. Learn to pray without ceasing but learn when to stop. Pray a matter three times and after that leave it, three times was enough for Jesus and for Paul. [3] Learn

---

3   This was also the practice of George Muller, although he prayed persistently for over 45 years for certain friends to come to the Lord. In matters of practical need he would bring his request 3 times and leave it to God's wisdom.

also as Jeremiah, to wait for the answer. [4]

You will also find many quotes from those Saints who prayed and have been given by God, through the risen Lord Jesus Christ to His Church to teach us and help us in our relationship with God. You will find, not so much of teaching us how to pray in this booklet, but rather teaching us how the Holy Spirit is the maker of true prayer and we need to be humble and listen to what others have learned concerning the place of the Holy Spirit in the offering of supplication to God.

Think of the need of the Holy Spirit but think also of what one is going to say, the best verses and promises to present to Him: The petition you are going to make, the pleas you are going to use and even the structure, but after everything always only resting on the Spirit's work. To offer one's prayers in such a way that correspond to the fact that *Majesty and honour are always to be before Him*.[5] The need for a sincere sense of the issues we are praying for. Mercy for the needs of the soul. Faith in the name of Jesus Christ.

---

4   Jeremiah 42.7
5   Psalm 96.6

A man may offer a prayer beautiful in diction and perfect in number of its petitions, but if it gives him gratification afterwards that prayer cannot have been truly prayed. C. Morgan

Notes for prayer

There are a number of *essential ingredients* needed for true prayer to be made to God and without which, it will be impossible to offer supplication before the throne of God. **(1)** The knowledge of the name of the High Priest who is seated at the right hand of the Father. *There is one mediator between God and men, the Man Christ Jesus.*[7] **(2)** For anyone to approach the holy God, the application of the blood of Jesus Christ in giving cleansing to the conscience is vital.[8] **(3)** The gift of the ministry of the Holy Spirit whose work it is to aid and help the offering of prayers according to the will of God because in our natural condition *we do not know what to pray for as we ought.*[9] **(4)** Faith: a belief that God is the rewarder of those who *diligently seek Him and without faith it is impossible to please Him.*[10] **(5)** The mouth to be filled with the Word of God so we may bring before Him His precious promises, that are *yea and Amen in Christ Jesus.*[11] **(6)** Real needs are vital for real prayer not to be a performance or an empty

---

7   1Timothy 2.5, John 14.13
8   Hebrews 10.22
9   Romans 8.26-28
10   Hebrews 11.6
11   2 Corinthians 1.20

act, desperate longings need to be expressed. **(7)** Consider seriously what you want, do not ask for things you do not desire or do not need. When you see what you want, keep to that and take heed to pray sensibly.

John Calvin highlights four practical ingredients in His teaching on the subject.

(1) *There must be a devout detachment required for conversation with God: Free from carnal cares.* Draw aside from distractions of pleasure and busyness to quiet the heart, do not be doing two things at once when speaking to the Great King. (Reverence)

(2) *To pray from a sincere sense of want and with penitence.* God is not interested with vain repetition. Pray for what one is burdened with; feels in the heart a pressing need in the moment of your personal concerns. (Reality)

(3) *Yield all confidence in yourself and humbly plead for pardon and mercy.* We are unable to produce one good petition in and of ourselves. (Repentance)

(4) Pray with confident hope, in the gracious will of God that all the promises are fulfilled in Jesus Christ. (Faith)

Praying well (Luther)

Do not bind yourself to words or symbol, but say one's prayers in one form today, in another tomorrow, depending upon mood or feeling. Study, however, as nearly as you can, with some general thought and ideas. It may happen occasionally that I may get lost among so many ideas in one petition you can forgo sixty others.

If an abundance of good thoughts comes to mind, we ought to disregard the other petitions make room for such thoughts. Listen in silence and under no circumstances obstruct them. The Holy Spirit Himself preachers here and one word of His sermon is better than a thousand prayers. You can learn many things more from one prayer, than you might have learned from reading and speculation.

Prepare your heart for prayer, do not jump from one

thing to another in one's thought when praying, for when it is all over, you do not know what you have done or talked about. It seems, says Luther, *that if we could see what arises as prayer from a cold and un-attentive heart, we would conclude that we had never seen a more ridiculous kind of buffoonery.*

But praise God it is now clear to me that those who forget what they said have not prayed well. In a good prayer one fully remembers every word and thought from beginning to the end of the prayer. Those who think of many things think *of nothing and does nothing right. How much more dear people, does prayer call for good attention, concentration and singleness of heart, if it is a good prayer.*

Pray as a justified sinner.

Remember you are in a fight against the devil and human weakness.

Don't despair or to try to escape. Instead lean into your needs.

Use the Bible as a prayer guide.

Hindrances and reasons to unanswered Prayer

Disobedient living produces extremely poor praying, no man can pray, really pray who does not obey.

E.M. Bounds

Christians can make many petitions but have few answers, or even no answer at all. If this is the case then consideration should be given to the reason why. Unanswered prayers do not give God the glory He deserves, knowing that God delights to hear and answer His children's requests. Prayers which give the most glory to God are not the most eloquent ones but answered prayers.

If I regard iniquity in my heart, the Lord will not hear. (Psalm 66.18)

They will call upon me, but I will not answer; They will seek me diligently, but they will not find me. Because they hated knowledge and did not choose the fear of the LORD. (Proverbs 1.28-29)

The Lord is far from the wicked, But He hears the prayer of the righteous. (Proverbs 15.29)

Whoever shuts his ears to the cry of the poor will also cry himself and not be heard. (Proverbs 21.13)

One who turns away his ear from hearing the law, Even his prayer is an abomination. (Proverbs 28.9)

Therefore if you bring your gift to the altar, and there remember that your brother has something against you, leave your gift there before the altar, and go your way. First be reconciled to your brother, and then come and offer your gift. (Matthew 5.23)

Let him ask in faith, without doubting, for he who doubts is like a wave of the sea driven and tossed by the wind. For let not that man suppose that he will receive anything from the Lord. (James 1. 5-7)

You ask and do not receive, because you ask amiss, that you may spend it on your pleasures. (James 4.3)

...that your prayers may not be hindered. (1 Peter 3.7)

Thoughts on the subject:

Be sure that you pray for nothing that is disagreeable to His will, err in judgment and passion – for it is a most vile abuse of God to beg of Him to do the devil's work.

O God never hear my foolish prayer, O God never hear my wicked prayer! O God never hear my proud prayer! O God never hear my angry prayer only hear such prayers as for thy glory and for thy good.

C.H. Spurgeon

Cold prayers shall never have any warm answers. Cold prayers always freeze before they reach heaven.

Thomas Brookes

Notes for prayer

Encouragement for Prayer

One of the best ways to offer prayers that are delightful and more according to God's will and mind is to take the Word of God in your hand and then place it on the lips in petitions to God. The best way of doing this is simply to read the Scriptures through which God speaks to you concerning the person of His beloved Son and His kingdom and that corresponds to the situation in which you may find yourself as a child of God. The Christian knows often of God speaking through His Word providentially. The best thing the Christian can do at this point is take that Word, it is not given by chance, it is a Word that is filled with God-given promises into the very situation you are experiencing. Realise nothing is by coincidence in this world, especially your reading of Scripture, so take of that Word and bring it to God and you will be offering petitions that are filled with His thoughts and desires, to which He delights to hear and finds it hard to resist in the reality of the present moment of need.[12]

These few verses are only a selection taken from

---

12   Mark. 7.27

God's Word to encourage us to pray, believing He hears your cry.

Likewise, the Spirit also helps us in our weakness. For we do not know what we should pray for as we ought but the Spirit Himself makes intercession for us with groanings which cannot be uttered. (Romans 8.26)

Now this is the confidence that we have in Him, that if we ask anything according to His will, He hears us. And if we know that He hears us, whatever we ask, we know, that we have petitions that we have asked of Him. (1 John 5.14)

And whatever you ask in My name, that will I do, that the Father may be glorified in the Son. If you ask anything in My name I will do it.
(John 14. 13-14)

For we do not have a High Priest who cannot sympathise with our weaknesses, but was in all points tempted as we are, yet without sin. Let us therefore come boldly to the throne of grace, that we may obtain mercy and find grace in time of need. (Hebrews 4. 15-16)

Let us draw near with a true heart in full assurance of faith, having our hearts sprinkled from an evil conscience and our bodies washed with pure water. (Hebrews 10.22)

But without faith it is impossible to please Him, for he who comes to God must believe that He is, and that He is a rewarder of those who diligently seek Him. (Hebrews 11. 6)

When you pray go into your room and when you shut the door, pray to your Father who is in the secret place and your Father who sees in secret will reward you openly. (Matthew 6.6)

But on this one will I look on him who is poor and of a contrite Spirit, and who trembles at My word. (Isaiah 66.2)

Other references:

1 Chronicles 4.10; 5.20.

Psalms 34.6; 37.5-6; 50.15,23; 81.10; 91.15; 96.6; 107.8-9; 136.1; 116.2; 118.27; 141.2.

Isaiah 40.31; 55.6-7. Jeremiah 33.3. Daniel 9.17-19 Zechariah 12.10.

Matthew 5.6; 6.5-8; 7.7-12; 9.38; 15.25; 18.20; 21.13.

Mark 11.23-24; Luke 11.1; 9-13; 18.13-14; 22.40; John 15.16; 16.23.

Romans 8.32; 10.12-13; 15.30; 12.1-2.

1 Corinthians 14.5. 2 Cornithians 1.11. Ephesians 3. 14-20; 6.17-19.

Philippians 1.4; 4.6; 4.19. Colossians 4.2.

1 Thessalonians 5.17; 1 Timothy 4.4-5; Hebrews 5.7; 11.1; James 5.13- 16; 1 Peter 5.7.

A Few verses to pray

God also has given us His Word not only to create faith to pray, or to instruct us to pray, but also to give our prayers words and arguments and promises and petitions to bring before Him. Every promise in the Bible is not only an invitation to pray but a command to pray according to the will of God. God will have impressed on your heart at some time a verse that you can speak to Him and bring before Him. These next few verses are some petitions recorded for us in Scripture, that we know for certain can be presented before God.

Let the words of my lips and the mediation of the my heart Be acceptable in your sight, O Lord, my strength and my redeemer. (Psalm 19.14)

Say to my Soul, I am your salvation. (Psalm 35.3)

Be exalted, O God, above the heavens; let your glory be above the earth. (Ps 57.11)

Oh, restore us again! (Psalm 60.1)

Strengthen, O God, what you have done for us. (Psalm 68.28)

Save me O God! For waters have come up to my neck. (Psalm 69.1)

Oh, do not remember former iniquities against us! Let Your tender mercies come speedily to meet us, For we have been brought very low. (Psalm 79.8)

Restore us, O God of hosts; cause your face to shine, And we shall be saved. (Psalm 80.7)

Do not forsake the works of Your hands. (Psalm 138.8)

Search me, O God and know my heart, Try me, and know my anxieties; And see if there is any wicked way in me, And lead me in the way everlasting. (Psalm 139.23)

O Lord, I said you are my refuge, My portion in the Land of the living. (Psalm 142.5)

Revive me, O Lord, for Your name's sake! (Psalm 143.11)

Cry out for discernment, And lift up your voice for understanding. (Proverbs 2.3)

Two things I request of you...remove falsehood and lies far from me, Give me neither poverty nor riches - feed me with the food you prescribe for me. (Proverbs 30.7-8)

Ask for the old paths, where the good way is. (Jeremiah 6.16)

Turn us back to you, O Lord and we will be restored, renew our days as of old (Lamentations 5.21)

Take away all iniquity; Receive us graciously, For we will offer the sacrifices of our lips. (Hosea 14.2)

Spare your people O Lord and do not give your heritage to reproach. (Joel 2.17)

O Lord, revive your work in the midst of the years! In the midst of the years make it known; in wrath remember mercy. (Habakkuk 3.2)

Ask the Lord for rain in the time of the latter rain. (Zechariah 10.1)

Therefore pray the Lord of the harvest to send out labourers into the harvest. (Matt 9.38)

Pray for those who spitefully use you. (Luke 6.28)

I pray for them. I do not pray for the world but for those whom You have given me, for they are Yours…I do not pray for these alone, but also for those who will believe in Me through their word. (John 17. 9,20)

Now I pray to God that you do no evil. (2 Corinthians 13.7)

that utterance may be given to me, that I may open my mouth boldly to make known the mystery of the gospel. (Ephesians 6.18)

I pray, that your love may abound still more and more in knowledge and all discernment… (Philippians 1.9-11)

that God would open to us a door for the word, to speak the mystery of Christ. (Colossians 4.3)

perfect what is lacking in your faith? And may the Lord make you increase and abound in love to one another and to all. (1 Thessalonians 3. 10 -12)

That our God would count you worthy of this calling and fulfil all good pleasure of His goodness and the work of faith with power, that the name of our Lord Jesus Christ may be glorified in you, and you in Him, according to the grace of our God and the Lord Jesus Christ. (2 Thessalonians 1.11- 12)

That the word of the Lord may run swiftly and glorified, just as it is with you, and that we may be delivered from unreasonable and wicked men. (2 Thessalonians 3.1-2)

Remember the prisoners as if chained with them. (Hebrews 13.3)

Pray for us; for we are confident that we have a good conscience, in all things to live honourably. (Hebrews 13.18)

If any of you lacks wisdom, let him ask of God, who gives liberally and without reproach and it will be given to him. (James 1.5)

Pray for one another that you may be healed. (James 5.16)

Maranatha. (1 Corinthians 16.22) Even so, come, Lord Jesus! (Revelation 22.20)

Notes for prayer

Some directions for prayer

One request we can offer to our Great High Priest, Jesus Christ, is *Lord teach us to pray.*[13] The request one disciple of Jesus asked on behalf of all disciples. If anyone comes to Jesus Christ there will be a hungering to know how and what to say to God. There is the realisation that without Jesus we are unable to even ask as we ought and we need Jesus to teach us. The Lord's prayer is given to us directly from that request; *Lord teach us to pray.*

And there is no greater instruction given than this taught by the Lord Jesus. There are many books written on the subject and we give thanks for such instruction given by teachers of the Church. Yet if we do pray neglecting what the Lord Jesus has, taught then it is foolish in the extreme and even full of pride, to think we know of a better method or manner of pleading with God. No, in all the great works of Church teaching such as the confessions, theological institutes and catechisms, virtually all contain instruction on the Lord's prayer.

---

13   Luke 11.1

In this prayer Jesus is not teaching us a prayer but how to pray, which is another thing altogether! Spurgeon said *"Men may as well speak to the moon thinking they will be heard as just repeating this prayer with no thought."*

The Lord never wanted His disciples to simply repeat words mechanically or even a method to follow but rather a manner, in knowing what prayer is. Richard Baxter, when giving instruction on the subject wrote the **first** ingredient needed for the Christian is that they believe this prayer, that what Jesus taught is good, there is not anything lacking or wrong in what Jesus taught. **Secondly,** the Christian needs to see that this prayer is necessary, it is not just one of many instructions given to us on how to pray but this one is to be believed, loved and cherished. **Thirdly,** this prayer is a commanded *prayer.*

In using the Lord's prayer try not to be taken up so much with simply saying the words but rather the spirit of the words. True communion rests on knowing a relationship with God, we call Him *Our Father,* we have the *Spirit of adoption,* we belong into His family and we are coming before the great

King as a child comes to a parent. There is the *spirit of adoration, hallowed be thy name;* if there is a structure to follow in prayer then it is to seek God's glory and God should always be the first thought of all our devotion. We need in prayer always the *spirit of submission, it is thy kingdom come, thy will be done,* true prayer is an offering up to God things that are agreeable to His will. Jesus prayed, *"Father, if it is Your will remove this cup from Me; nevertheless, not My will but Yours be done."* F. B. Meyer's prayer was *"Make me willing."* We need also the *spirit of supplication,* the last thing we need in prayer is to become so spiritual that we do not ask for anything (the devil would love it), *you do not have because you do not ask,*[14] we are to *open our mouth wide*[15] and not only for the spiritual needs but for our daily bread and the necessities of life. C.S. Lewis in his book Prayers to *Malcom, 'you must pray for the physical needs of people. You cannot bypass it only caring for the soul it is unreal it is not true.'* The spirit of forgiveness is needed, *forgive us our trespasses as we forgive them that trespass against us.* We sin every day, people will sin against

14   James 4.2
15   Psalm 81.10

us every day, we need forgiveness every day, we need to forgive every day. The last petition to carry with us into prayer is the *spirit of godly fear*.

I want a principle within of jealous godly fear; A sensibility of sin a pain to feel it near. I want the first approach to feel of pride, or wrong desire; To catch the wandering of my will and quench the kindling fire.

Charles Wesley.

The simplicity and profundity of this prayer is staggering in what it teaches us concerning God, with a mind that is conscious of our need, confessing sin, continuing daily to depend on Him, bending ourselves to conformity to His will. There is a beautiful balance in its structure, God is always first, then human needs, it is for the spiritual as well as the practical, it is not only praying for oneself but others.

We are called to pray for one another. John Calvin made the request *Lord save us from being self-centred in our prayers, and teach us to remember others*. What better answer to our problem when bringing our requests to pray the words *'for us.'*

Not forgetting the great Amen. As your Amen is so has been your prayer.   Martin Luther

<u>See that you understand the use and ends of prayer</u>.

Labour – to know above all the God to whom you pray - Maker, Redeemer, Owner, Ruler, Father.

Labour – when you are to pray, stir up your soul and belief of unseen things.

Labour – for a constant acquaintance of oneself, your sins and manifold want's and necessities, to know what they are.

Labour hard - with all your heart to keep, reverent, serious, fervent.

Honour God in prayer with reverence. Address Him in the manner as your Heavenly Father. Make petitions worthy of a great King. Praise Him in the name of His beloved Son Jesus Christ the Lord.

Notes for prayer

Practical Considerations

We are both body and soul united. What we do with our body effects our spirit: *you were bought at a price; therefore glorify God in your body and in your spirit, which are God's.* [16]

Standing – (Nehemiah 9.5). Kneeling – (Ezra 9.5). Sitting – (1 Chronicles 17.27). Bowing – (Exodus 34.8). Hands lifted up - (1Timothy 2.8). Eyes lifted up – (John.17.1). I beseech you therefore brethren by the mercies of God, that you present your bodies a living sacrifice, holy acceptable to God which is your reasonable service. (Romans 12.1)

Places of prayer

In the secret place – (Matthew 6.6). Family – (Acts 10. 2,30). Public – (1 Corinthians 14.14-17). The upper room - (Acts 1.13-14). In house - (Acts 12.5.17). By river – (Acts 16.13). On beach – (Acts 21.5). Everywhere - (1 Timothy 2.8)

---

16   1 Corinthians 6.20

Jesus prayed

Early in the morning – (Mark 1.35). At His baptism – (Luke 3.21). At night – (Luke 6.12-16). In public – (Matthew 11.25). On the mountain - (Luke 9. 29). With others – (Luke 11.1). In the garden - (Mark 14.32). On the cross - (Luke 23.34).

Jesus commands

Asking – receiving. Seeking – finding. Knocking - opening. (Matthew 7.7-8)

Notes for prayer

Public Prayer

Not everyone who comes to a prayer meeting is sincere about prayer, but those who are sincere concerning prayer will be at the prayer meeting.

If my people who are called by my name will humble themselves and pray and seek my face and turn from their wicked ways than I will hear from heaven, and will forgive their sin and heal their land. (2 Chronicles 7.14)

And He said to them, it is written, My house shall be called a house of prayer. (Matthew 21. 13)

You also, as living stones, are being built up a spiritual house, a holy priesthood, to offer up spiritual sacrifices acceptable to God through Jesus Christ. (1 Peter 2.5)

These all continued with one accord in prayer and supplication, with women and Mary the mother of Jesus, and with His brethren. (Acts 1. 14)

It is said by many who never attend a prayer meeting, or if they do it may be once a year, *that prayer is the power house of God, or that a Church marches on its knees!* Saying catch phrases as these about prayer or even believing such things concerning prayer will not change a thing no matter how much we believe what we have said, unless we PRAY. Make the most of every opportunity when one is called upon to make intercession. Do so, knowing that every request is to be meaningful in the plan and purpose of God. There is only one thing worse in quenching prayer in the life of the body of Christ than not attending the Church's prayer meeting and that is to attend it and not pray. What a waste of the glorious privileges which belong to the Christian in Christ Jesus. It is bad enough to disobey God's will by keeping away from the means of grace when we are commanded to do so, but not to make any petition, not one, when in a prayer meeting is like a child who defies the Father's will to His face, He says call on me and the sinful heart says *"no."*

Prayer meeting prayers[17]

1) Prayers should be short or of moderate length. Long prayers however excellent are wearisome and quench the spirit of direction.

---

17 Thoughts gleaned from John Angell James on Church membership.

2) The prayers should vary, there is no need for each to cover all topics. Let the first prayer be of personal experience or the needs of the present. Secondly, to enlarge upon the affections of the Church, Ministers, families, work. Thirdly, mission, confession, thanksgiving for mercies, petitions and need of blessings.

3) Prayers should be loud, but not so loud as unpleasant, they should be reverent and absent of telling God what to do.

4) Avoid all poetry and all indifferent words of repetition, phrases such as we *beseech thee*.

5) When prayer is coming to an end it should not be renewed again because something additional comes to mind.

6) Prayers are to be *prayers* and not preaching. John Owen gives three simple directions for the public prayers of the Church – the Word of God and the success of it in ministry. The presence of Christ to be among His people. The needs of the congregation.

<u>Pray short</u> – *to give others in the meeting opportunity to pray. It is necessary to draw near unto God. But it is not required of you to prolong your speech till everyone is longing to hear the word. Amen.* C. H. Spurgeon

<u>Pray loud</u> – because we are praying not on our own but to God along with others who can add the Amen to the cry we along make, to do this they must be able to hear the petitions made.

<u>Pray in unity</u> – do not pray for everything that pops into one's head believing it is of the Holy Spirit, rather there is the unity of the Spirit who leads and brings the minds and hearts of God's people to be united in their devotion and love and concern for the things of God. The prayer meetings that have known the Spirit of God at work are marked by uniting the petitions made to God by His Spirit.

<u>Pray big</u> – do not use the public prayer meeting for the small requests, we can bring all our anxieties to Him but there are great petitions and needs of the corporate body of Christ, ask for conversions, reviving of God's people, power and success on

the ministry of the Word, the condition of the Church, the coming of Jesus Christ.

<u>Pray in faith</u> – every prayer must be carried to the Father with a believing heart that God is able to do more than we ask or think. *Believing prayer never asks more than is promised.*   William S Plumer

<u>Pray for others</u> – do not pray for self but to pray for others. Samuel Rutherford said, *"I have been benefited by praying for others; for by making an errand to God for them I have gotten something for myself."*

<u>*PRAY*</u> – Just pray.

Notes for prayers

Problems of public prayer meetings

There is no other meeting in Church life that is more attacked than the prayer meeting. Fact. If you doubt such a statement it may be due to the reality that you do not frequently attend such a meeting. As soon as you consider prayer being of the utmost importance you soon become aware of every obstacle in your path from family, friends, Christians, work, pleasure, unseen emergencies, illness; the devil himself does all he can to hinder this work of the Church.

The prayer meeting can be the devil's battlefield. His attention is focused on this one place in any Church, no matter how small, the moment God's people begin to call on Him. The devil has little concern of what happens in the social centres in the community such as sports and secular events. His guns are pointed at the prayer meeting and if he can't stop God's people from going to the meeting the next step is to stop the mouth of those who attend the meeting, he is more active in this meeting than any other.

If the devil cannot stop the Christian from going or even from praying at the prayer meeting, the prayer meeting may become not only the devil's battlefield but the devil's playground. He is delighted and over-joyed at the end of any prayer meeting that has been used up in speaking to the Almighty God great doctrines of faith. The devil knows all these truths better than any Christian and if only he can make the believer say long prayers without ever making a mere request, it has been a good night at the prayer meeting for him and his cause, another meeting where answers will not be found because no requests are made. But the devil hates and trembles, not so much at the weak believer on their knees but the weakest believer making even the feeblest request in and through the mighty name of Jesus. But if the devil cannot stop the request his next tactic is to lead the meeting to ask amiss. How when great needs are to be made before the Great King, we ask for so little? We can pray for the government but should we not pray for the Gospel first which has the only power to change the lives of men and women. We pray for sinners needing to be saved but was not the Lord's first prayer in John 17, for the ones His Father had given that they may be a means to bring those who were *to believe in His name*. We pray for the physical and there is need to do so but should not the spiritual sickness of the soul not be the greatest concern, an eternal destiny at stake?

If the devil cannot stop all of this then the next step is to lead to an expression of excess and to kindle a false fire. But the devil is not to have the blame in everything, so often we hear the excuses not to pray based on feelings, yet the Lord has commanded us to call on Him. To say that we do not feel moved or led, especially in the light of His command, the desperate need around us of lost men and women who do not know God, is not a spiritual position to take but a sinful one of disobedience before God and hardness of heart before one's neighbour.

Notes for prayer

To pray with the Spirit

*Praying always with all prayer and supplication in
the Spirit. (Ephesians 6.18)*

Praying in the Holy Spirit. (Jude 20)

*No prayer is made on earth alone, the Holy Spirit
pleads.*[18] People can and have given themselves
to the life of devotion but no prayer can be made
without the Holy Spirit. If we do not trust in the
office of the Holy Spirit in prayer, we will go down
the path of vain ideas, human learning and all the
dead practices of human tradition.

Then on the other hand, no one has control over
the Spirit of God, *the wind blows where he wishes.
Who has directed the Spirit of the LORD, or as His
counsellor taught Him?*[19] There is no system or
teaching anyone can give and make the claim
do this, follow this, and you will know what it is to
pray in the Spirit. What we can consider is the fact
of what God has said to us concerning the work of
prayer, that this work is one in which the Holy Spirit
of God is to be most active and engaged with in

18   James Montgomery
19   Jon 3. 8, Isaiah 40.13.

aiding the saints to *make intercession according to the will of God.*[20] The blessed third person of the Holy Trinity is given the great work of applying the great blessings of the Gospel to our lives and one of these blessings is that He aids, gives the impulse and kindles a sacred flame of incense on the altar of our hearts to give thanksgiving and petitions unto God the Father. The promise of the Gospel is that God will pour out *the Spirit of grace and supplication on His people.*[21]

Now with this being the case, that God's Spirit is given to us for this work as the Scriptures have clearly declared and that although there is nothing we can do to establish a method, or manner of means that will bring Him down upon our supplications, the one thing we can do is not to deny Him His place and role in this work in the first instance. To pray in the Spirit is to look to Him; we would seek His face and ask for His ministry to be outworked in our lives; that He would fulfil His great work on and in our lives, say to Him *Oh Spirit come,* it is vital we have our prayers heard and that they be according to His great will. Give Him this

---

20   Romans 8.26,
21   Zechariah 12. 10.

rightful role and do not give it to another.

It is easier to explain what praying in the Spirit is not, it is not praying a set format of printed prayers constructed by any Church. Praying in the Spirit is never leaning on our own ability and memory to pray without our written manuscript according to the skills we may naturally have. To pray in the Spirit is not to pray any outward form of structure that we may think is even Biblical; *where the Spirit of the Lord is there is freedom.*[22] A need may drive us to our knees, burdens and anxiety can overwhelm us, but to pray in the Spirit is not to be bound in anyway by our needs or forms of prayer, written prayers or even pressures to pray from outside. Circumstances may bring us to call on God so often as expressed by the Psalmist, but to pray in the Spirit is to be lifted up from all these things and to be taken up with another view of God. To pray in the Spirit is not only to know what to pray for but how not to.

What little advice we could give is to be careful not to quench the Spirit with any set forms of written or unwritten rules we may have constructed but

22   2 Corinthians 3.17

rather give thanks to God for the help He has provided and to look to Him in the name of Jesus.

Understand that God does expect from us our thanksgiving, praise and confession and God commands us to do so. We are to do this not out of feeling and praying only when we are moved but of obedience to His command.

An indication of praying in the Spirit is praying with an understanding of those things we ask, *the Spirit gives birth to spirit.*[23] *For If I pray in a tongue, my spirit prays, I will pray with the spirit, and will also pray with understanding.*[24] Another aspect will be of things brought to remembrance, promises of Scripture, the goodness of God in our lives, sins of the past, the needs of the saints.[25] A freedom and also a feeling in our natural affections of love for God, sorrow for sins, a crying with the voice, an urgency of the need. In such a prayer there should then be a spirit of humility, of reverence and faith, forgiveness, simplicity, tenacity and expectation.[26]

---

23   John 3.6
24   1 Corinthians 14.14-15
25   John 16.15.
26   Luke 18.14; Matthew 6. 5-6,14; Luke 18.1-8

Remembering in each prayer we trust in His help and understand that according to His free will He gives more aid sometimes than others. We may struggle at times and our petitions seem like lead balloons and at other times they soar high like an eagle. We are not to take His work for granted. We need to treasure up and store matter for this duty in our devotionals, we need to think about His blessed promises, verses of scripture and requests. We need to ask and think what is acceptable to bring before Him and to diligently acquire to pray in the Spirit. *Prayer is the practice of prophesying to the wind.* [27]

---

27   Ezekiel 37.9

Some sayings on Prayer

God never denied that soul anything that went as far as heaven to ask for it. John Trap

To pray effectively we must want what God wants that, and that only, is to pray in the will of God. A. W. Tozer

Better to have heart without words than words without heart. John Bunyan

There must be fired affections, before our prayers will go up. William Jenkyn

All the prayers in the Scripture you will find reasoning with God, not a multitude of words heaped together. Stephen Charnock

Pray often rather than very long at a time. It is hard to be very long in prayer, and not slacken in our affections. William Gurnall

Prevailing prayer is almost an impossibility when there is neglect of the study of the Word of God. R.A Torrey

True prayer does not preach to God, it does not lead by the hand, but reaches for the guiding hand.

Prayer conjoins holy reverence and holy familiarity with holy boldness.

True prayer shows God the divine hand writing of Scripture and the divine signature of His covenant promises.

Prayer has an unexplainable way of argument both the worthiness of Christ and unworthiness of the sinner, hence it is both the chief part of humility and thankfulness.

Prayer honours God, acknowledge His being, exults His power, adores His Providence, secures His aid. E. M. Bounds

May it be the real I who speaks, may it be the real thou that I speak to. C.S. Lewis

Prayer is good, the habit of prayer is better but the spirit of prayer is best of all. C. H. Spurgeon

Printed in Great Britain
by Amazon